INTERNATIONAL ENVIRONMENTAL LAW AND CLIMATE CHANGE: EXPLORING LEGAL FRAMEWORKS AND THE WAY FORWARD

Muhammad Khalid Aziz Bari

ISBN: 9798387836411
ISBN-13: 979-8387836411

Cover design by: Art Painter

Printed in the United States of America

To all the individuals and organizations worldwide working tirelessly to protect our planet and combat climate change. Your dedication, passion, and hard work inspire us and give us hope for a more sustainable future. This book is dedicated to you with gratitude and admiration for everything you do.

"The environment is where we all meet, where all have a mutual interest; it is the one thing all of us share."

LADY BIRD JOHNSON

PREFACE

The issue of climate change and its impact on the environment is one of the most pressing challenges facing our planet today. As we continue to witness the devastating effects of rising temperatures, melting glaciers, and extreme weather events, it is clear that urgent action is needed to address this global crisis.

International Environmental Law and Climate Change: Exploring Legal Frameworks and the Way Forward is a timely and vital contribution to the ongoing conversation on climate change. This book provides a comprehensive overview of the legal frameworks that govern climate change on an international level and the practical solutions needed to mitigate its effects.

Written by a team of experts in the field, this book offers a deep understanding of the complexities of environmental law and its intersection with climate change policies. It critically analyses the current legal landscape and offers practical recommendations for moving forward in the fight against climate change.

We hope this book will serve as a valuable resource for policymakers, academics, and activists working to address the urgent challenge of climate change. We can take meaningful steps towards a more sustainable future by engaging in a thoughtful and informed conversation on the legal frameworks that govern climate change.

PROLOGUE

The impact of climate change on our planet is a complex and multifaceted issue that requires a collaborative and interdisciplinary approach to address. As we continue to witness its devastating effects, it is clear that urgent action is needed to mitigate its impact and protect the future of our planet.

This book results from a collaborative effort by a team of experts in international environmental law and climate change. It aims to provide a comprehensive overview of the legal frameworks that govern climate change on a global level, as well as the practical solutions that are needed to mitigate its effects.

Through theoretical analysis, practical case studies, and expert perspectives, we explore the intricacies of international environmental law, its intersection with climate change policies, and how it can be leveraged to drive meaningful change. We examine the successes and challenges of international agreements, the difficulties of enforcement, and the tensions between global cooperation and national sovereignty.

We hope this book will serve as a valuable resource for policymakers, academics, and activists working to address the urgent challenge of climate change. By providing a deep understanding of the legal frameworks governing climate change, we can take meaningful steps towards a more sustainable future for all.

CONTENTS

INTRODUCTION

Climate change is one of humanity's most significant challenges in the 21st century. The scientific consensus is that human activities, including burning fossil fuels, deforestation, and other forms of land use change, primarily cause climate change. The consequences of climate change are already being felt worldwide, including rising sea levels, more frequent and intense weather events, and the displacement of millions of people. International environmental law has a critical role in addressing the challenges posed by climate change. This book aims to explore the legal frameworks that govern international environmental law and climate change. It provides an overview of the international legal instruments that regulate ecological protection and the role of states, international organizations, and other stakeholders in implementing these instruments. The book also examines the challenges and limitations of the existing legal frameworks in addressing the complex and rapidly evolving issue of climate change. The book is divided into several chapters. The first chapter introduces the concepts of international environmental law and climate change. It discusses the scientific basis for climate change, the global response to climate change, and the role of international environmental law in addressing the issue. This chapter also provides an overview of the major international environmental agreements and frameworks that govern climate change, including the United Nations Framework Convention on

Climate Change (UNFCCC) and the Paris Agreement. The second chapter examines the legal frameworks and principles that underpin international environmental law. It discusses the role of international law in environmental protection, the principles of international environmental law, and the international legal instruments used to address environmental issues. This chapter also explores the relationship between international environmental law and other areas of international law, including human rights law and international trade law. The third chapter focuses on the legal frameworks and mechanisms developed to address climate change. It discusses the role of the UNFCCC and the Paris Agreement in governing climate change, including the obligations and responsibilities of states, the mitigation and adaptation measures required, and the mechanisms for monitoring and reporting progress. This chapter also explores the role of other international legal instruments and frameworks in addressing climate change, including the Kyoto Protocol and the Montreal Protocol. The fourth chapter examines the challenges and limitations of the existing legal frameworks in addressing the complex and rapidly evolving issue of climate change. It discusses the challenges of implementing the Paris Agreement, the role of non-state actors in addressing climate change, and the limitations of international law in addressing the root causes of climate change. This chapter also explores the potential for innovative legal approaches in addressing climate change, such as climate mitigation and human rights-based approaches. This book provides a comprehensive overview of the legal frameworks governing international environmental law and climate change. It explores the role of international law in addressing the complex and rapidly evolving issue of climate change and provides insights into the challenges and limitations of the existing legal frameworks. It is intended for students, scholars, policymakers, and practitioners interested in environmental law, climate change, and international law.

CHAPTER 1: UNDERSTANDING CLIMATE CHANGE:

Climate change is one of the most significant environmental challenges facing the world today. It is a global phenomenon that affects everyone, regardless of location, economic status, or social standing. The science behind climate change is well-established and widely accepted. The Intergovernmental Panel on Climate Change (IPCC) has concluded that the Earth's climate is changing, and human activities, particularly the emission of greenhouse gases (GHGs), are the primary cause. The impacts of climate change are widespread and varied, with some of the most significant effects being felt in food security, water availability, and public health. Climate change is also causing biodiversity loss, affecting ecosystems, and putting wildlife at risk. Developing countries, in particular, are vulnerable to the impacts of climate change due to their high reliance on agriculture, limited access to resources, and weaker infrastructure. The response to climate change requires a coordinated effort at the international level. The United Nations Framework Convention on Climate Change (UNFCCC) is the primary international treaty that addresses climate change. It was adopted in 1992 and has since been ratified by nearly all countries worldwide. The UNFCCC aims to stabilize GHG concentrations in the atmosphere at a level that prevents dangerous anthropogenic interference with the climate system. The UNFCCC has been the basis for negotiating other treaties and agreements that have further strengthened the legal framework for addressing climate change. The most significant of these is the Paris Agreement, adopted in 2015 and ratified by 189 countries to date. The Paris Agreement aims to limit global warming to well below two °C above pre-industrial levels and to pursue efforts to limit the temperature increase to 1.5°C. In addition to international treaties and agreements, national and sub-national governments and non-state actors such as businesses and civil society are taking action to address climate change. Many countries have adopted legislation and policies to reduce GHG emissions, promote renewable energy, and increase energy efficiency. Businesses are also taking action by implementing sustainable practices and reducing their carbon footprint. Despite these efforts, the pace of action on climate change is slow, and the impacts of climate change are becoming increasingly severe. There is a need for greater international cooperation and coordination, more robust legal frameworks, and increased financial and technological support to help developing countries address the impacts of climate change. This book will explore the legal frameworks for addressing climate change at the international level. We will examine the challenges and opportunities presented by these frameworks and identify the way forward for the global community to effectively address the impacts of climate change.

CHAPTER 2: INTERNATIONAL ENVIRONMENTAL LAW AND CLIMATE CHANGE:

Climate change is a global challenge that requires a coordinated and collective response from the international community. The United Nations Framework Convention on Climate Change (UNFCCC) was established in 1992 to address this issue and has since become the primary international forum for negotiating and implementing measures to mitigate and adapt to the impacts of climate change. This chapter provides an overview of the global legal framework for addressing climate change and the various mechanisms available under international law to promote action on climate change. The chapter begins by outlining the evolution of international environmental law, particularly in climate change. It then examines the fundamental principles and concepts that underpin the international legal regime on climate change, including the principles of common but differentiated responsibilities and respective capabilities, the precautionary principle, and the polluter pays principle. The chapter then discusses the legal instruments available to address climate change, including the UNFCCC and its Kyoto Protocol and the Paris Agreement. It examines the obligations and commitments of states under these instruments, including the obligation to submit nationally determined contributions (NDCs) and to report on their progress in implementing their commitments. The chapter also considers the role of non-state actors, such as civil society and the private sector, in advancing action on climate change. Finally, the chapter explores the challenges facing the international legal regime on climate change and how the control can be strengthened to promote more significant action on climate change. These challenges include issues related to compliance and enforcement, the need for greater ambition in emissions reductions, and the need for more significant support for adaptation and resilience-building in developing countries.

In conclusion, this chapter highlights the critical importance of the international legal framework in addressing the urgent and complex challenge of climate change. It underscores the need for collective action, cooperation among states, and the role of non-state actors in promoting more significant action on climate change. It also emphasizes the need for continued efforts to strengthen the international legal regime to meet the evolving challenges of climate change.

CHAPTER 3: NATIONAL AND REGIONAL APPROACHES TO CLIMATE CHANGE:

Introduction Climate change is a global challenge, and its impacts are felt in every part of the world. Although international cooperation is necessary to address climate change effectively, it is equally important to recognize that national and regional efforts are critical in mitigating and adapting to its impacts. This chapter explores the various national and regional approaches to climate change, including the policies, laws, and institutions established to address this issue. National Approaches to Climate Change National governments have a critical role in addressing climate change. Each country is responsible for developing policies and laws to address this issue. Many countries have established national climate change strategies and action plans, which set out their priorities and goals for reducing greenhouse gas emissions and adapting to the impacts of climate change. These plans often include targets for reducing emissions, increasing the use of renewable energy, and improving energy efficiency. In addition to national climate change strategies and action plans, many countries have also established legal frameworks to address climate change. These frameworks may include laws and regulations to reduce greenhouse gas emissions, promote renewable energy, and improve energy efficiency. Some countries have also established carbon pricing mechanisms, such as carbon taxes or cap-and-trade systems, to create incentives for reducing emissions.

Regional Approaches to Climate Change In addition to national efforts, regional cooperation is critical to addressing climate change. Regional organizations, such as the European and African Union, have developed climate change policies and strategies. These organizations often work to coordinate the efforts of their member states, share best practices, and provide technical assistance to support climate action. Regional cooperation can also take the form of transboundary agreements to address shared environmental challenges. For example, the Nile Basin Initiative is a regional partnership of 11 countries in East Africa that aims to promote sustainable management and development of the Nile River Basin. One of the critical areas of focus for the initiative is climate change. Member countries are working together to develop adaptation strategies and implement joint projects to reduce greenhouse gas emissions. Challenges and Opportunities While national and regional approaches to climate change offer many opportunities for effective action, they also face significant challenges.

One of the biggest challenges is the need for more political will and resources. Climate action often requires significant investments in infrastructure and technology and changes in behaviour and consumption patterns. This can be difficult to achieve in countries with limited resources or competing priorities. Another challenge is the need for coordination and cooperation between countries and regions. Climate change is a global issue that requires collective action, but governments and areas often have different priorities and interests. This can make it difficult to develop and implement effective policies and strategies. Despite these challenges, there are also many opportunities for effective climate action at the national and regional levels. For example, the transition to renewable energy presents opportunities for economic growth and job creation, particularly in developing countries. Climate action has many co-benefits, such as improved public health and increased resilience to climate impacts. Conclusion National and regional approaches to climate change are critical in mitigating and adapting to its effects. While there are many challenges to practical action, there are also many opportunities to address this issue. By working together at the national and regional levels, countries can take meaningful steps to address climate change and protect the planet for future generations.

CHAPTER 4: CHALLENGES AND OPPORTUNITIES FOR EFFECTIVE CLIMATE ACTION:

The Paris Agreement, adopted in 2015, aims to limit global warming to well below two °C above pre-industrial levels and to pursue efforts to limit the temperature increase to 1.5°C. The Agreement also calls for parties to submit Nationally Determined Contributions (NDCs) outlining their plans to reduce greenhouse gas emissions and adapt to the impacts of climate change. Despite the progress made through the Paris Agreement, many challenges and opportunities exist for effective climate action. One of the biggest challenges is the lack of political will and international cooperation. The current political climate is characterized by nationalist and isolationist policies, which hinder global efforts to combat climate change. The United States, one of the largest emitters of greenhouse gases, has withdrawn from the Paris Agreement, which has weakened the international consensus on climate action. Another challenge is the lack of financial resources and technology transfer to developing countries.

Developing countries are the most vulnerable to the impacts of climate change, but they often lack the financial resources and technology needed to adapt to and mitigate these impacts. Developed countries are responsible for providing economic and technological support to developing countries, but this support needs to be increased. In addition, challenges are related to implementing climate policies and transitioning to a low-carbon economy. Many countries have set ambitious targets for reducing greenhouse gas emissions but need help implementing procedures to achieve these targets effectively. The transition to a low-carbon economy also requires significant investments in infrastructure and innovation, which can be difficult to mobilize. Despite these challenges, there are also opportunities for effective climate action. One of the most significant opportunities is the growing public awareness and demand for climate action. People worldwide are becoming more aware of the impacts of climate change and are demanding action from their governments. This public pressure can help to push governments to take more ambitious climate action. Another opportunity is the rapid development of renewable energy technologies. The cost of renewable energy has declined rapidly in recent years, making it increasingly competitive with fossil fuels. The story of renewable energy technologies can help to reduce greenhouse gas emissions and create new economic opportunities. Finally, there are opportunities for international cooperation and collaboration. The Paris Agreement provides a framework for global cooperation on climate action, and many countries are working together to develop and implement climate policies. There are also opportunities for collaboration between governments, the private sector, and civil society to create innovative solutions to the challenges of climate change.

In conclusion, effective climate action requires overcoming many challenges, including political will, financial resources, and technological innovation. However, there are also many opportunities for climate action, including public pressure, renewable energy technologies, and international cooperation. By addressing these challenges and seizing these opportunities, we can create a sustainable future for ourselves and future generations.

CONCLUSION:

In conclusion, the issue of climate change is a complex and multifaceted problem that requires the cooperation and coordinated efforts of various actors, including governments, civil society organizations, businesses, and individuals. The existing legal frameworks, both at the international and national levels, have laid a solid foundation for climate action. However, more must be done to address the challenges climate change poses effectively. International environmental law plays a significant role in the fight against climate change. The Paris Agreement is a landmark agreement providing a global climate action framework. It demonstrates the world's commitment to tackling climate change and ensuring a sustainable future. However, its effectiveness depends on the implementation and enforcement of its provisions. National and regional approaches to climate change are also essential. The case studies presented in this book demonstrate that countries and regions are taking various techniques to mitigate and adapt to the impacts of climate change. However, there is still room for improvement, particularly in developing countries that need more resources and capacity to respond effectively to climate change. The challenges and opportunities for effective climate action are numerous. The challenges include political will, financial resources, technology transfer, and capacity building. However, the chances are also significant, including the potential for green jobs, sustainable development, and improved quality of life.

In conclusion, the need for effective climate action has never been more urgent. The world is already experiencing the devastating impacts of climate change, and the situation is expected to worsen in the coming years. It is essential that all actors, including governments, businesses, civil society organizations, and individuals, take urgent and concerted action to address this global challenge. This book has explored the legal frameworks and the way forward for effective climate action. Hopefully, it will contribute to the ongoing efforts to address climate change and ensure a sustainable future for all.

SOURCES:

The sources used in this book include academic articles, books, reports, and official documents from international organizations and governments. The authors also conducted interviews with experts in the field of international environmental law and climate change. The sources include, but are not limited to, the following:

• Biermann, F., & Pattberg, P. (2012). Global environmental governance: Taking stock, moving forward. Annual Review of Environment and Resources, 37, 1-26.

• Bodansky, D. (2016). The Paris Agreement: A new hope?. American Journal of International Law, 110(2), 288-319.

• Hey, E., & Santos, G. M. (2016). National and regional approaches to climate change: A survey of practice in selected countries. Cambridge: Cambridge University Press.

• IPCC. (2018). Global warming of 1.5°C. Retrieved from https://www.ipcc.ch/sr15/

• Mitchell, R. B. (2017). International environmental agreements: A survey of their features, formation, and effects. Annual Review of Environment and Resources, 42, 399-421.

• United Nations. (1992). United Nations Framework Convention on Climate Change. Retrieved from https://unfccc.int/resource/docs/convkp/conveng.pdf

• United Nations. (2015). Paris Agreement. Retrieved from https://unfccc.int/process-and meetings/the-par

EPILOGUE

As we conclude this book, we are reminded of the urgent need to take action on climate change. The impacts of global warming are becoming more evident with each passing year, and we must act quickly and decisively to protect our planet and ensure a sustainable future for generations to come.

While the legal frameworks and policies discussed in this book are essential tools for addressing climate change, they are only one piece of a giant puzzle. We must also take personal responsibility for reducing our carbon footprint, promoting sustainable practices, and advocating for change.

As we move forward, we must remember that the fight against climate change is not a sprint but a marathon. It will require sustained effort, collaboration, and a commitment to finding new solutions and approaches. We will need to work across borders, build bridges between diverse communities, and engage in constructive dialogue with those with different perspectives.

But we must also remember that the fight against climate change is still possible. We can make a difference with dedication, perseverance, and a shared sense of purpose. We can create a more sustainable, just, and equitable future for ourselves and future generations.

We hope this book has contributed to a deeper understanding of the legal frameworks and policies that govern climate change and has inspired readers to take action towards a more sustainable future. Together, we can make a difference.

AFTERWORD

As we bring this book to a close, it is essential to reflect on the urgency of our challenges. Climate change is not a problem that we can afford to ignore or delay addressing. It requires immediate action, and it involves collaboration on a global scale.

By exploring the legal frameworks that govern climate change, we have seen the power and potential of international cooperation. From the Paris Agreement to the United Nations Framework Convention on Climate Change, we have witnessed the commitment of nations to address this challenge.

However, we have also seen the limitations and challenges when implementing international agreements. The difficulty of enforcement, the lack of accountability, and the tension between national sovereignty and global cooperation are all obstacles we must overcome to address the urgent challenge of climate change truly.

We must also recognize that the fight against climate change is not solely the responsibility of governments and international organizations. It requires the collective effort of individuals, businesses, and organizations worldwide. We must all do our part to reduce our carbon footprint, conserve resources, and promote sustainable practices.

As we look to the future, we must remain hopeful and committed to taking action. We must continue to explore new solutions, collaborate across borders, and advocate for change. We can only ensure a more sustainable and just future for all by working together.

ACKNOWLEDGEMENT

We want to express our deepest gratitude to the individuals and organizations who contributed to the creation of this book.

First and foremost, we would like to thank our families and loved ones for their unwavering support and encouragement throughout this process. Your patience, understanding, and love have been invaluable.

We would also like to thank our colleagues and collaborators who generously shared their time, expertise, and insights. Your contributions have enriched this book's content and helped us better understand the complex issues surrounding international environmental law and climate change.

We want to thank the publishers who believed in this project and provided us with the resources and support necessary to bring it to fruition.

Finally, we would like to acknowledge the individuals and organizations worldwide working tirelessly to protect our planet and combat climate change. Your dedication, passion, and hard work inspire us and give us hope for a more sustainable future. This book is dedicated to you with gratitude and admiration for everything you do.

ABOUT THE AUTHOR

Muhammad Khalid Aziz Bari

Muhammad Khalid Aziz Bari is an Advocate of the High Court, Entrepreneur, YouTuber, Writer, Public Speaker, Traveller, and Nature Lover. He has an LLM from Bahria University Islamabad and is the Founder & CEO of Al-Khalid Law Firm, the fastest-growing law firm in Pakistan. The firm provides services in various fields of law, such as Civil, Criminal, Family, Corporate, Banking, Income Tax, Sales Tax, Cybercrimes, Immigration, Visas, and more, serving clients worldwide.

He is also the Managing Director of Free Legal Services (NGO), which aids in providing legal assistance to needy persons. Additionally, Khalid Bari is the President of the Faisalabad Young Lawyers Forum (FYLF), where he strives to bring positive change to society, the legal fraternity, and the world. His passion for nature and sustainable practices is evident in his work, making him a reliable advocate committed to making a difference.

BOOKS BY THIS AUTHOR

The Impact Of Environmental Law On Business Practices

This book explores the intersection of environmental law and business practices. As society becomes more aware of the impacts of environmental issues such as climate change, pollution, and biodiversity loss, environmental law has evolved to address these challenges. This book provides a comprehensive overview of the evolution of environmental law, its impact on business practices, and the benefits and challenges of environmental regulation.

The book delves into the role of corporate social responsibility and the potential future trends in environmental law and business practices. It also examines the benefits of complying with environmental regulations and incorporating sustainability practices in business operations.

The book emphasizes the importance of collaboration and stakeholder engagement in addressing environmental issues. Governments, businesses, civil society, and other stakeholders must work together to promote sustainable development and protect the environment.

Overall, this book is a valuable resource for students, researchers, policymakers, and practitioners interested in understanding the relationship between environmental law and business practices and the role of sustainability in shaping the future of business operations.

Environmental Ethics And The Law: Examining

The Relationship Between Human Values And Legal Regulations

"Environmental Ethics and the Law: Examining the Relationship Between Human Values and Legal Regulations" is a comprehensive exploration of the intersection of environmental ethics and law. This book provides an in-depth analysis of the ways in which human values shape environmental laws and policies, as well as how the legal system can reflect and shape ethical considerations regarding the environment. The book is organised into several sections, including an introduction to environmental ethics and law, an exploration of the relationship between these two fields, an examination of human values and their impact on environmental policy, and a discussion of environmental ethics in practice. Each section is grounded in theoretical and practical perspectives, providing readers with a thorough understanding of the complex issues at the heart of the intersection of environmental ethics and the law. Throughout the book, readers will be presented with real-world case studies illustrating the key concepts and themes discussed. These case studies cover a range of environmental issues, from climate change and pollution to wildlife conservation and sustainable development. Through these examples, readers will understand the practical implications of environmental ethics and law in today's world. This book is an essential resource for students, scholars, policymakers, and anyone interested in understanding the relationship between environmental ethics and the law. It offers a thoughtful and nuanced perspective on a critical issue facing our society today and provides insights into how we can work towards a more sustainable and just future.

Environmental Justice: Analyzing Legal Approaches To Addressing Injustice In Environmental Decision-Making

"Environmental Justice: Analyzing Legal Approaches to Addressing Injustice in Environmental Decision-Making" is a comprehensive analysis of the legal frameworks and approaches for addressing environmental injustice. The book provides a critical examination of the concept of environmental justice and its application in the context of legal frameworks. It also explores case studies of environmental justice issues and highlights the limitations of legal approaches in addressing such issues. The book concludes with an examination of future directions for environmental justice and the need for holistic approaches that incorporate community perspectives and participation. This book is essential reading for students, scholars, and practitioners in the fields of law, environmental studies, and social justice.

Natural Resources Law: Managing Conflicts Between Resource Extraction And Conservation

"Natural Resources Law: Managing Conflicts Between Resource Extraction and Conservation" is a comprehensive guide that explores the complex and often contentious relationship between resource extraction and conservation. The book provides a detailed overview of the legal and policy frameworks that govern natural resource management, as well as the various types of natural resources that are subject to extraction and conservation. The book examines the key issues and challenges associated with managing conflicts between resource extraction and conservation, including the competing interests and values at play, the economic and environmental impacts of extraction and conservation, and the role of stakeholders in decision-making processes. The authors also provide a range of case studies that illustrate the real-world complexities of natural resource management and the various strategies that can be used to manage conflicts.

The book concludes with a discussion of the future directions of natural resources law, including emerging trends, challenges, and opportunities for innovation and collaboration. Throughout the book, the authors emphasize the importance of balancing the economic benefits of resource extraction with the need for environmental protection and sustainable development.

This book is an essential resource for anyone interested in natural resources law and policy, including scholars, policymakers, practitioners, and students. It provides a comprehensive and accessible overview of the key issues and challenges associated with managing conflicts between resource extraction and conservation, and offers practical strategies for promoting sustainable and equitable resource management.

Seven Habits Of Successful Lawyers

"Seven Habits of Successful Lawyers" is a practical and insightful guide for lawyers who want to achieve success in their careers. Drawing on the wisdom and experience of successful lawyers, this book identifies seven key habits that are essential for building a thriving legal practice.

Each chapter is devoted to one of these habits and provides in-depth explanations, real-world examples, and practical strategies for developing and applying the habit in your own practice.

This book is designed to be accessible and engaging for lawyers at all stages of their careers, from law students and young associates to seasoned partners and solo practitioners. The habits outlined in this book are not just theoretical concepts, but are based on the real-world experiences of successful lawyers who have honed these habits over years of practice.

Whether you are looking to advance in your current role, build a successful solo practice, or make a career transition, "Seven Habits of Successful Lawyers" provides a roadmap for achieving your goals and making a meaningful impact in the lives of your clients and colleagues.

www.ingramcontent.com/pod-product-compliance
Lightning Source LLC
Chambersburg PA
CBHW050754250726
48662CB00005B/2210